On Beyond a Million

Million

An Amazing Math Journey

David M. Schwartz

illustrated by Paul Meisel

BANTAM
SCHOOL
VISITORS
PARKING

DRAGONFLY BOOKS®
NEW YORK

For my sister, Judy,
who's one in a million
and beyond
—D.M.S.

For my dad,
who gave me an
appreciation of math
(and tennis)
—P.M.

Published by Dragonfly Books®
an imprint of Random House Children's Books
a division of Random House, Inc.
1540 Broadway, New York, New York 10036

Text copyright © 1999 by David Schwartz
Illustrations copyright © 1999 by Paul Meisel

Visit us on the Web! www.randomhouse.com/kids

Educators and librarians, for a variety of teaching tools, visit us at
www.randomhouse.com/teachers

Cataloging-in-Publication Data is available from the Library of Congress.
ISBN: 0-385-32217-8 (trade)
0-440-41177-7 (pbk.)

The text of this book is set in 15-point One Stroke Script.

Book design by Semadar Megged

Reprinted by arrangement with Doubleday Books for Young Readers

Printed in the United States of America

November 2001

10 9 8 7 6 5 4 3 2 1

Assembly Today
Professor X and his dog, Y
What's going on?
We can't stop this thing!
We'd better stop it or we'll drown.
Yeah, but how do we turn it off?

Did you know?

5 people are born on Earth every second.

A spider has 8 legs.

About 100 acres of tropical rain forest are destroyed every minute.

150 little brown bats fit easily into a backyard birdhouse.
One hundred.
100
Hey, how did you get to a hundred so fast?
It took me fifteen seconds to count to a hundred by ones, and I'm fast! You can't just go one, ten, one hundred!

Did you know?

The Sears Tower in Chicago is 110 stories high.

The U.S. Postal Service delivers 200 pieces of junk mail every second.

It has been 400 years since rain has fallen in the driest place on Earth, the Atacama Desert of Chile.

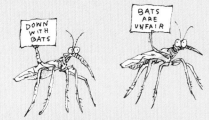

One little brown bat can snap up 600 mosquitoes per hour.

There are about 1,000 hairs on a square inch of your head.

Giant tortoises can weigh 500 pounds or more. During the age of sailing ships, sailors kept them in the holds, where they could survive for more than a year.

Did you know?

The oldest trees on Earth are about 2,200 years old.

To taste your food, you use 9,000 taste buds on your tongue.

There are 40,000 different characters in Chinese, while our alphabet has only 26 letters.

If all the veins in your body were stretched out in one line, they would extend 70,000 miles.

100,000 people worked 20 seasons to build one pyramid.

About 2,500 types of flowering plants live in a plot of Amazon rain forest that you could walk around in 15 minutes.

10 x 10 x 10
There are about 60,000 bees in a hive.
One hundred thousand.
Now we're multiplying five tens together—that's 10^5.
10^5
ONE HUNDRED THOUSAND
10 x 10 x 10 x 10 x 10

Did you know?

There are 400,000 hairs on a square inch of a sea otter's pelt.

One colony of weaver ants contains 500,000 ants. They weave nests out of leaves in the treetops.

If everyone in the United States recycled their newspapers, we would save 500,000 trees every week.

Up to 1,000,000 (one million) leaf-cutter ants can live in one colony. They can strip rain forests of their leaves and destroy croplands overnight.

A square yard in the rocky area of seashore between high tide and low tide may be home to 900,000 animals.

Thanks a million, Professor X. You're one in a million!

It only took us six counts!

That's because a million is 10^6. That means a one with six zeros.

A million is the same as a thousand thousand. A thousand is $10 \times 10 \times 10$, and if we multiply that by another thousand, or $10 \times 10 \times 10$, we have
$$10 \times 10 \times 10 \times 10 \times 10 \times 10 = 10^6 = \text{One Million!}$$

Hmmm. So $10^3 \times 10^3$ is the same as 10^6? All you have to do is add those little exponents together and you get your answer: $10^3 \times 10^3 = 10^6$. Easy!

Cool!

Did you know?

If you doubled a penny every day, after 30 days you would have a total of $10,737,418.23 (ten million, seven hundred and thirty-seven thousand, four hundred and eighteen dollars and twenty-three cents).

Every day, 37,000,000 (thirty-seven million) Tootsie Rolls come rolling out of the factory.

On your sixth birthday you have lived 189,216,000 (one hundred eighty-nine million, two hundred and sixteen thousand) seconds.

There are about 250,000,000 (two hundred fifty million) people in the United States today.

Americans eat about 500,000,000 (five hundred million) pounds of popcorn each year.

228,000,000 (two hundred twenty-eight million) years ago, the dinosaurs appeared.

Ten million, one hundred million, one billion.

Yeah, how high can we go?

$10 \times 10 \times 10$ (a thousand) times

$10 \times 10 \times 10 \times 10 \times 10 \times 10$ (a millio is

$10 \times 10 \times 10 \times 10 \times 10 \times$ $10 \times 10 \times 10 \times 10$ (a billion).

That's the same as $10^3 \times 10^6 = 10^9$.

A TRILLION

= ONE MILLION MILLION

= 1,000,000,000,000

= 1,000 X 1,000,000,000

= 1,000,000 x 1,000,000

$= 10^3 \times 10^9 = 10^{12}$

$= 10^6 \times 10^6 = 10^{12}$

= 10 x 10 x 10 x 10 x 10 x 10
x 10 x 10 x 10 x 10 x 10 x 10

Did you know?

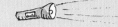

Light travels about 6,000,000,000,000 (six trillion) miles in a year. That distance is called one light-year.

There are 10,000,000,000,000,000,000,000 (ten sextillion) atoms in every breath you take.

The Earth weighs about 13,000,000,000,000,000,000,000,000 (thirteen septillion) pounds.

3×10^{72} (3 × 1,000,000,000,000,000, 000,000,000,000,000,000,000,000, 000,000,000,000,000,000,000,000, 000,000,000) is the approximate number of atoms in the universe, according to some scientists. But no one really knows.

The Sun gives off as much light as 6,000,000,000,000,000,000,000,000 (six septillion) 60-watt lightbulbs.

Quadrillion, quintillion, sextillion, septillion, octillion, nonillion, decillion . . .

Look, the numbers are growing by powers of one thousand. Each one is a thousand times bigger than the last one.

This is even faster than Power Counting.

It's Super Power Counting!

Let's Super Power Count to infinity!

You can't count to infinity, no matter how powerfully you do it.

These numbers are so long, it takes forever to write all the zeros. That's why scientists use exponents. Look at how much easier it is: 10^{68} instead of 100,000,000,000,000,000,000, 000,000,000,000,000,000,000, 000,000,000,000,000,000,000, 000,000

How do you say

79,538,387,920,
899,947,
478,111,348,
980,792,404,040,199,
479,138,555?

79 quindecillion,
538 quattuordecillion,
387 tredecillion,
920 duodecillion,
899 undecillion,
947 decillion,
478 nonillion,
111 octillion,
348 septillion,
980 sextillion,
792 quintillion,
404 quadrillion,
40 trillion,
199 billion,
479 million,
138 thousand,
five hundred
fifty-five.

10^{100}

is a lot easier to write than

10,000,000,000,
000,000,000,000,
000,000,000,000,
000,000,000,000,
000,000,000,000,
000,000,000,000,
000,000,000,000,
000,000,000,000,
000,000.

It says here that a mathematician wrote a one followed by a hundred zeros. He showed it to his young nephew, who said, "Googol!" Ever since then, a one with a hundred zeros has been called a googol.

Do you think anyone in the world has a googol dollars?

Not even a googol ants in the world?

Not even a googol specks of dust in the atmosphere (and in my room!)?

Then what good is a googol?

I know! Let's have googol-writing contests with our friends. We'll let them write out all the zeros, and when they get to the ninety-eighth zero, we can just write 10^{100} and win!

I don't think so. It says there isn't a googol of anything.

Nothing.

Nothing. Not even a googol atoms in the universe!

I guess a number that big isn't good for much. It's just fun.